Dear Jack —
   How lovely to see you again
and deliver this personally.
We'll be ordering your Cat book
and look forward to the one
after. Fondly, Kate
PS: Thanks for the cricket education.
googly has a brand new meaning!

What Snakes Want

TO
Peter, for unconditional love
and
Robin, for believing in this book

What Snakes Want

Poems by
Kita Shantiris

Mayapple Press 2015

Published by   Mayapple Press
                       362 Chestnut Hill Road
                       Woodstock, NY 12498
                       www.mayapplepress.com

ISBN 978-1-936419-51-7

Library of Congress Control Number 2015901667

Acknowledgments:

Grateful acknowledgment to the following publications where
these poems first appeared, sometimes in slightly different forms:
Afterimage, The Alley Cat Readings 5, Ambit, The Border (Bomb-
shelter Press), *Crannóg, The Fish Anthology,The Little Magazine,
The Moth, ONTHEBUS, Poetry & The Modern Language Association,
Quarterly West, Slipstream, Snap, Wisconsin Review.*

Special thanks to Jack Grapes and Michael Andrews of Bomb-
shelter Press; Donald Justice for his encouragement after Squaw
Valley; Dan Menaker for his support; W. S. Merwin for answering
my letters; Uncle Elias Schwartz for decades of feedback; and Judy
Kerman and Mayapple Press for believing in this book.

My thanks also to Clem Cairns, Patrick Chapman, Vievee Francis,
Amy Gerstler, Ed Harris, Alice Jones and my faithful readers —
especially Laura Darlington and Charlotte Fletcher.

Cover design by Judith Kerman based on zoological prints by Al-
bertus Seba. Book design and layout by Judith Kerman with text
and titles in Book Antiqua. Author photo by Laura Darlington.

Contents

I   1

Beyond Fort Worth   3
The Fall   4
Consonants   5
That Which Is Wanting   6
Girls' Hobbies   7
Homage to Gilberto Guidarelli   8
Three Chairs in Creel, Mexico   9
No Te Preocupes, Blanca   10
The Laundromat on the Road to Nirvana   11
Rickrack   12
Gratification   13
As Close As I Can Come to a Love Poem
    with Three Sides   14
Ansel Adams' Calendar   15
What Snakes Want   16
Goethe's Girdle   17
Rounding Out   18
Detour   19
Chameleon   20
Travelers' Scrabble   21
The Last Lake   22
The Weight of Snow   23
Doubt   24
Scars   25
Black Lake   26
Remedy   27
Nightlight I   28

II   29

Nightlight II   31
Rear View Mirror   32
The Border   33
Searchlight   35
Groundwork   36
Chagall's Village   37

Making Sparks   38
The Builder   39
Lactarius Deliciosus   40
The Good Guy   41
My Racy Mind   42
Parsing The Body   43
Pair-Bonding   44
Oranges   45
The Ledge   46
An Honest Moon   47

III   49

Pins   51
Theft   52
Henry Darger's Faith   53
The Shelf Life of Grief   54
P.O. Box 434   55
Jettison   56
Fabric   57
Handiwork   58
Swing Low Sweet Chariot   59
Hope Is a Thing with Feathers   60
Darting Light   61
Lures   62
Tuning the Sails   63
Maidenhair Trees   64
Four-Letter Words   65

Notes   66
About the Author   67

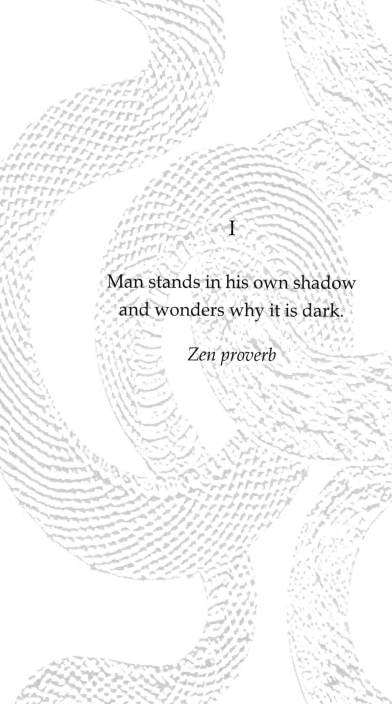

I

Man stands in his own shadow
and wonders why it is dark.

Zen proverb

Beyond Fort Worth

Mama killed a chicken snake
and tarantula. She wrapped us
in blankets before the tornado.
Come morning, everything
that was tall had fallen.
One tree. The brick chimney.

Every window was squint.
The dust insidious.
I wrote *clean me*
on the Venetian blinds.
Mama sliced her thumb
washing them with ammonia

in the same bathtub
where the dog quivered
when he heard thunder.
When Mama heard gravel,
she knew what it meant.
She knew my father's engine,

how dust accelerates.
There was no good reason
for him to come home early
or my brother to draw
deserts without people.
No good reason for me

to yearn in the scrub
for another dose of sunset.
If I pushed up a chair,
I could reach Mama's pills
for blood poisoning.
They were yellow like candy.

The Fall

Not the brilliance of October
but the descent from a limb —
like a leaf changing into a verb.

Like crows succumbing
to the West Nile Virus.
So many gone now, so many

dead on the ground, no longer
connecting subject and predicate.
As if they were punished

for relishing success,
for crowing with raucous joy.
So sad how verbs evolved

for the birds and the beasts.
How it's unseemly
to dog the one you love.

The horse shakes its mane
and becomes a boy
in the principal's office.

A boy who smells the world outside
and wants to race in the grass
and be rewarded

with a hand full of sugar.
Not the hard note home
or the hand that will hurt him.

A boy that still has the lungs to crow
but could so easily
be broken.

Consonants

The H is silent in Hermés.
All those silk tongues
in your father's tie rack.

Not like the S in scream. Yours
when you found your mother
asleep in a tub of red water.

Sometimes the W is silent.
It was when she shouted
whore across her DMZ,

forbidding you from crossing
to the family with Legos.
You didn't hear their TV

spreading lies about her,
didn't want to play
with fire or mumbly pegs.

All you wanted
was to build forts
on their spotless parquet.

That Which Is Wanting

This is a song for the weight
of your laptop and backpack
on your flight to the Canaries.

For all birds, which defy gravity,
and for your eyes, which I hope
will also rise again—

A song for Señora Perez
who will gather her skirt around her knees
and meet you at low tide

where she will teach you to prepare
sea snails in slimy mouthfuls
al mojo de ajo.

For vino tinto on the table
and the heater that warms everyone
under the wings of the tablecloth.

A song for the farmhouse you will rent
beside the culvert and the bananas
it irrigates. For the stone wall

where men will sit watching you,
like livestock whose heat no longer rises
from the stalls beneath your floor boards.

A song in the key of red.
The tip of their cigarettes
at the edges of dawn and twilight.

The long draws at their lips,
embers waxing and waning.
They, too, feel the wind. They hear

the call and answer of the ocean.
They, too, are waiting for it to return
everything it has taken.

Girls' Hobbies

Some fit into jodhpurs
and learn to whip,
to curry and cool down
after gallops. Or

they arrange figurines
and dream
how the horse prances
threatening those bucks

that make riding half luck
and final triumph.
Yes. To rein in to the tether
still on top. And oh

what fodder for the boys
who watch legs spread
for long accelerating trots,
girls leaning to nuzzle

their geldings' wet necks.
It makes the boys forget
the stall, the dismount—
it makes the boys forget

horses don't ride,
they carry.

Homage to Gilberto Guidarelli

[A statue in Ravenna's Palace of Fine Arts]

For centuries librarians and teachers
have bought nighties on special
packing for luck in Ravenna.
Heels skimming museum tiles, they arch
slim wrists over bannisters rising
to kneel at your chiselled lips.

These are not heroines to undo
your death. They would trade
their stockings for a lobster
but no brokers come to strip their sleep
so they kiss you and wish.
Send them husbands or happiness.

Gilberto, your hat's tipped.
Have you been wicked?
After your fatal duel with Orsini,
Benita commissioned this image.
Did she ask for that war-blade
between your hips?

Could she foresee the typists?
Last year, to avoid the stain
of lips, the curators had you wrapped
in plastic — see through —
but oh, the chants and pickets!
Now janitors swab you with Purex.

Poor Gilberto, turned
from knight in Federico's court
to pawn in ladies' romances.
At night they hide in the curtains
hoping to have you alone after six.
Wishes are truth, truth wishes.

That is all they know on tour
and all they need to know.

Three Chairs in Creel, Mexico

One white, two not,
each chair has a heart wrought
in its open back. The black shadow
of the white chair's seat is touching
the solid leg of its companion.
This heat exaggerates dimensions.
Focus on the man in the middle.
He's flanked by the señora he already has

and the tourist he's always envisioned.
Because the world reverses in everyone's lens,
his dreams lengthen with each inch
he touches of her lacy hem.
He's settled in his burnished seat
but he can also imagine
a world curved like a peach
beyond his horizon.

No Te Preocupes, Blanca

Don't worry
if Baja burns for you.
The baker will give you all
his warm bolillos
because you are whiter
than the coals
in his abuelo's oven.

Y no te preocupes
if Pepe takes you to sea
libre. He won't be surprised
if you don't let him rub you
with Aztec sunscreen.
He is a going to sing
at the rudder anyway.

And if the road slows
to red flags and dust?
Ahead twenty men will be following
an oil truck shoveling pebbles,
but don't worry Mamacita.
They'll just kiss-kiss
stroking your white Pinto.

Also, here roosters crow
all night, Blanca.
After the day's siesta
of hot corn and gravel,
even an ankle of moonlight
is inspiring.
Sueños dulces.

No te preocupes.
Mañana,
shoulders blistered,
only embroidery will hurt you
squatting in Pasadena
scrubbing tar
off the fender.

The Laundromat on the Road to Nirvana

Its walls are splashed with paradise —
Hawaii, Tahiti, Micronesia —
you can get there in hours.
The way is your choice
between stewardesses' outfits.

Pink foam curlers, poppin' Bazooka,
the woman who brought five loads
in two garbage cans
is folding Jockey shorts
beneath a discreet side shot
of Bali topless.

Santa Monica's guru is stripping
to his last sheet
in front of the jumbo washer.
A Delta gazelle beckons in her mini skirt.
The mere spin of my jungle print brassiere
could give you wanderlust.

Stop in any hour.
The sign for new whirlpools means
washes have gone up a quarter.
Still, unless your wet stuff is very heavy,
a few bucks will do everything.

Rickrack

My mother and Kay were divorcées
back when the word was full of innuendo.
When single men had Corvettes
and women wore two-piece bathing suits.
I scowled when they sat on men's laps
sipping martinis out of pitchers.

The bachelors hired me to clean
shaving scum from their basins.
I didn't bill them for reading
the dirty parts in *Lolita*
but nothing could hide what I did
to Mr. Chandler's miniatures.

I just wanted a little sip of his gin.
Who knew the seals would snitch?
When I turned sixteen, I fit
into Kay's hand-me-downs.
I found myself wanting Skip
to explore the rickrack neckline

on her seersucker dress,
to go places I couldn't mention.
Instead, he drove 100 miles an hour
while I begged him to stop —
not knowing we'd never go
farther or faster.

Gratification

My lover brings *Playboy* to bed with us.
He touches himself spying on our neighbor.
Every morning on my way to class
some man slams his window up

holding his stalk like a flower.
Like that man when I was 12
asking for directions. All roads led
to the thing in his lap he was waving.

The next year, Jimmy Olson grabbed
my budding silhouette at the corner.
I don't really recall his name —
only his hands and the shame

but someone deserves credit.
I've had it. I'm staking out the lot
that's known for its campus flasher.
Not to catch *him*. To reap

what I've sown with my professor.
I'm ready for his Harley.
If he lets me steer his hands,
I'll lie down like a map.

As Close As I Can Come to a Love Poem
with Three Sides

Let's forget equations,
which sides add up,
whether to square distance.
You are the given —
my deceptive fact.

Something proscribes us
like a rusty compass.
Let's put miles between us
and that circumference.
The road is our ruler.

Medians divide our nights
into kisses. When we shift
in the dark, the constellations
split into pieces.
Under bleached motel sheets

I dream of desks collapsing,
classes I never attended,
someone with protractors
slashing the curtains.
I'm beginning to envy

objects that pivot —
rail crossings, scissors,
bolts that aren't frozen.
Things that work just two ways
have only one answer.

Ansel Adams' Calendar

After March
I didn't expect April
to look like this.
I'm facing thirty days
without buds or dew.
Just a dead trunk
and its consequences
shot in brutal light.

What Snakes Want

Mama, you tell me
you paid for my overbite.
It wasn't worth it.
You tell me I still have
the tongue of a serpent.
Let me tell you what snakes want.

Only their weakness for milk
brings them down
from the gnarled rock slopes.
Something in their flat heads
senses the odor.
They will crawl on their long bellies

across the shadow of a threshold.
They will find nursing mothers,
the damp lips of infants.
They will defy the splinters
of a cradle. They will. Mama,
I will defy you until you listen.

Goethe's Girdle

Nothing is more fattening than solitude.
My heart growls

stripping the cupboards.
Dear Wilhelm, I have tried

trading peristalsis for passion —
walnuts and sausage,

babka and schnapps — Homer
when my stomach balks.

Each word is a lump.
Let's not bite at my delusions.

If you could see me
in this orgy of distraction,

you'd say, my friend,
I want love too much.

No. I want too much
to be deserving.

Oh, if my blood were lighter.
I'd open a vein and float.

Rounding Out

Keep going. Let out your trousers.
Develop a fetish for condiments.
Follow each off-ramp to its griddle.
Every exit — a new soup du jour,
variations in house dressing.
Twenty-four hours a day,
someone will serve you pancakes.

So what if Coco's blender short-circuits?
The Denny's next door uses real ice cream.
Forget your heart and cholesterol.
Leave a trail of straws and broken cremoras.
Every bite puts more between you
and that scrawny perfectionist.
Nothing lasts except appetite.

Detour

Her booths tell fortunes
for a penny.
She serves cheap chili and refills
looking younger in her hairnet.
She changes the salt
to help time pass.

Everyone loves
spinning at the counter,
the green and chrome malt maker,
the way she blushes
when someone breathes her name
onto a window.

Everyone looks for her
when they don't want to make time.
Broke on lovers and atmosphere?
She'll wash your thermos.
It's the all-night café
going under off the interstate.

Chameleon

I should be bronze and indolent
down here by the equator.

The sea mocks what's green in me
so out of synch with the weather.

I jog trailing clouds of red dust.
There's no spring in my Nikes.

Bring on the bats and coyotes
a lethal sliver of the moon.

The sun can't disappear fast enough
to suit my shadow.

Travelers' Scrabble

A day strangers huddle together.
In a shirt so plush I could have
written on your back and chest,
you opened the board
and inverted each letter.

The wind blasted its say
on the shelter we'd pieced
from relic beach camps.
You said, *Like gauze, not suave,*
undoing my spelling.

Mauve. The exact tinge
of my Baja contraband.
Conch slippers steamed in vino,
spiny pincushions — blooming
in the dark wheel well.

The Last Lake

It gave you seven trout
without stealing one lure,
lifted my nipples higher
than your mouth could.
Six lakes fell from it
like dew in a web.
At night, the same vapors
that made sunset a splash
of fish and swallows
condensed as frost on our bags.
Ice plugged the canteens.
The dogs woke limping.
The second night we didn't touch
I'd have called the tears sweat
if you had asked.
At dawn we turned back,
blocked by the ridge and boulders.

The Weight of Snow

The sorcery
of spun sugar.
The tongue.

Breath
and the sky
colliding.

Velocity.
The impact
of white.

Drifts
at the door,
icy sheets.

Long nights,
an accumulation
of silence.

The roof
buckling
under the elements.

Doubt

Just when I'm dropping off
with Lao-Tzu propped on my pajamas,
some dusk turns physical.

I need a stronger master.
It takes brandy to center me
glowing alone here.

I can't rise and set
without desiring.
Nothing tugs like the Pacific.

I get dressed
and burn late on the pier
eyeing companions.

Is the sun really
just shining? Is it
oblivious to its conjunctions?

Just when I'm good at the lotus,
at one with each twig in the universe,
tattooed sailors pass.

Hearts darken their biceps.
They stare like they see something
in my position.

They act like I'm looking.

Scars

I'm looking for a photo of you from Burma.
One that was shot after combat.
One where your cheeks are lined
with sweat and fear like the treads
tanks make driving through mud.

Deep in the jungle, I'm looking for a way
to forgive you for the monsoons
and all you leeched from us.
Something to illuminate
the explosions that followed.

A way to forget all the nights
I pretended my bed was a ditch
and sleep had already killed me.
A way to forget you brooding in the doorway
like a panther in one of your war stories.

Someone inside me kept watch
while you taught us to make bedrolls
the way they taught you in the army.
If I didn't learn quickly, you might strike
with your unpredictable paw.

You waged hand-to-hand combat
with the furniture and anyone big enough
to question your authority.
Now you are a prisoner
of your wheelchair.

I'm going to push you as fast as I can.
It's time you knew how it felt
when you gunned that blue Ford to ninety.
You're not driving anymore.
You're mine for interrogation.

Black Lake

I found the faint trail through cedar,
went downwind on the toes of my lug soles.
Animals — were you sleeping?
Nothing but your droppings
under a manzanita.

I know you see me
sweeping with cedar,
clearing rocks for my soft body.
I know you will hunt while I sleep,
dreaming little clouds
out the pucker of my mummy bag.

Black Lake is fading.
Only stones hold the day in,
a little heat as the trees form
one great shadow.
Grease sets around the trout head
in my tin skillet.

I must sleep before the sun
leaves nothing. I must sleep
before the stars make themselves
visible. Anything dim
could get my heart going
just breathing in the bushes.

I'm afraid I'll wake
to something I can't see.
It will gnaw the ax by my hand
or lick me for salt
and my moustache of cocoa.
It will trample the glasses in my hiking boot.

The dark pushes me forward.
No fires on the opposite shoreline.

Remedy

Ishi's treatment for rattlesnake bite was to bind a toad
or frog on the affected area. — T. Kroeber, Ishi in Two Worlds

They say we are the apples of our parents' eyes
and when the wind blows, down will fall cradles.
My father was tied and whipped under a sycamore.
They say he almost smothered me smashing the playpen.

They say we marry our parents over and over.
Tonight I fear what crawls camped here in Joshua Tree.
The dark dives lower on bats' wings while the moon electrifies
each creosote — plants that thrive by leaking poison.

You shake our sleeping bag for scorpions.
I draw the top in tight. You drift between my thighs
until sleep slides a diamondback up my ankle.
Holy Cross, Cholla, Ocotillo. They say

snakes know their prey by motion. I wake screaming.
I'm paralyzed by these dreams over and over.
You say in some bedtime stories
the frog is a prince.

Nightlight I

Daddy's home.
Time to play possum.

Come morning
I don't want to wake up

to everything broken.
Don't want to bring him

tomato juice for his headache.
He's going to swallow the light

breathing in the doorway.
Listen. His shoes' rhythm.

When it stops, I know
he's deciding.

II

Hope is the thing with feathers
that perches in the soul.

Emily Dickinson

Nightlight II

You undress at the front door
because you know how I sleep,

set down your amp,
drop your clothes in a heap

and tiptoe through the house
already naked.

Still, I hear the tempo of your feet
feel the air change

when you enter our bedroom.
Sometimes I pretend to be asleep.

Sometimes I don't want anyone
blocking the light, not even you.

Rear View Mirror

You grabbed the past in your hands
by accident. You were looking straight ahead
as if nothing were in the mirror.

It had been a night of happy hallucinations.
Furniture in my front yard to make room for dancing —
windows wide open, hips slightly in synch,

sweat and reggae infecting everyone.
The cops called it disturbing the peace.
You split after we carried the bed in.

You'd almost made it to the off-ramp
when a black and white pulled even.
You smiled at the officers like you were innocent,

made a smooth move adjusting the mirror.
They laughed when it broke loose
and everything behind you fell into your lap.

The Border

We arrive at Gare du Nord in a snowstorm.
You are from my future life.
Everything has the grain
of old movies —
the great wheels,
the collapsible ladder
from the Pullman. Your face
is flecked and wavering.

You follow me to the bookstand
where shadowy things happen,
where spies know each other
by their magazines.
We both are looking for stories
to keep us occupied
on a long trip,
for the right person

to drop a ticket.
The clerk is suspicious
exchanging your currency:
When did your beard turn silver?
What was your name in Budapest?
I undo my hair at the landing.
Marble amplifies steps.
I'm afraid to look

over my shoulder.
It is you. You take my arm
at the Exit.
The sun is lost.
Grey monuments surround us.
We are mysteries
in our wintercoats.
You are thinking —

Black Irish
Icy eyes in this blizzard.

You feel years of flight
rush your breathing.
What is hidden
below my ruffles?
Why is my valise
ticking?

I search your eyes
for deceit.
For a man who squeezes
too hard coming
or a man who expects women
to unpack for him
confusing his heart
with a suitcase.

The future comes from behind us,
from the tiny projection room
and its hidden microphones.
It drives a black roadster.
We can shake it.
Any minute, rounding a corner,
aujourd'hui at noon in Paris—
we will speed toward the border.

Searchlight

The sun is holding its breath
like someone in bed listening
to what sounds like a burglar,
or a soldier about to play taps
or Gabriel muting his trumpet.

Today the sun is illuminating
everything dark under the bed,
every dent we ever made
without leaving a note,
every mote in our corners.

The sun is white pepper.
We'll sneeze if we stare.
Staring longer will blind us.
Not for touching ourselves
but for looking at heaven.

Today is the sun's longest.
So many hours until we sleep.
So few until we awaken.
Cover me like the month of June.
Gentle the insomnia of summer.

Groundwork

Armloads of knot grass,
scraps of roofing,
stems matted in the driveway —
all gone with the trashman
for a little I slipped to him.

To find the border
that has always been here,
I had to squat coaxing
each root system. I spit dust
when my tugs boomeranged.

I troweled up pill bugs
grey as my mind
curled into itself,
pocketed a green cat's eye
that made me feel chosen.

I studied the sun
crossing the shingles,
how the eaves deflect it.
Where I could not have my way
with the marigolds,

I learned begonias,
coleus, impatiens.
You will never see
what was weeded.
You will only feel

mine are the hands,
I used them.

Chagall's Village

It was the year of the June eclipse.
The first time I saw Bella's corona.

Her hands were zinc white like her neck.
Never chapped from milking.

I lived on the outskirts of her circle.
I could tell you that I sat at her side

and milked her, that I thrummed with the crickets.
I could lie. We could lie in the fields

until her father took his scythe and shaved them.
Mathematicians would call our love

a truth-set.   An intersection
of amethysts and herring.

Bella smelling of the lilac light
and of me and my village.

Making Sparks

No fire was ever made so—
not from two sticks
just rubbing.
There's no magic
in saplings.

It takes a hearth,
dry but not brittle,
soft for a notch
where the drill fits.
Even poison oak will catch.

Dig a moat at right angles
to the hearth's inlet.
Line it with lichen, thistledown,
the innerbark of a willow.
Concentration is the secret.

Only so can the arm twirl
long enough and fast enough
to heat rivers of sawdust.
First brown, then brighter,
something red ignites in the tinder.

The Builder

You lose yourself in your wrist
and grip. I know by the sounds
you make pounding. You take
small nails and work them

before the actual screw or pin.
Your final twists are quick.
I want you to master
the dying art of joinery.

Planks flush in mortises and lap joints,
Japan's temples outlive dynasties.
Swelling with each whisper of humidity,
creaking through every tremor,

their old kneecaps never collapse.
It starts when masters enter the forest —
blessed, blessing pine and cedar —
pulling the saw towards their hearts.

Lactarius Deliciosus

Consuela's house was forgiving.
In spite of its tile floors,
no one was afraid of broken glass
or of wine turning violent.
She grew up with a full basket
of apples and cheese,
faith in tradition.
Every fall, her family spread its blanket
under the gold chestnut trees.

Light reached through the leaves
and blessed her father's mushroom knife.
All around, families were singing
of torn hunks of bread
that fit together and olives
cured after they fell from the tree.
It was a medley of novenas
blessing their hunt for saffron milk caps
and the feast that would follow.

The Good Guy

Darling, you're predictable
as Bonaparte for the canvas.
Count all the times you've leaned forward,
the same arrangement of elbow and knee,
jaw set half-smiling. It leaves me uneasy —
like dark that's too quiet

or a long spell of unbroken dishes.
Our album could illustrate a story.
Mt. Lassen, Las Vegas, the family graveyard —
your pose recurs like the white hat
in a cowboy movie. It reduces our vacations
to backdrops that move behind the actor.

We judge the hero by his hat.
I've ceased to notice the moods
around your mouth and eyes,
whether the down on your body is backlit.
I see a posture repeating itself.
Looking at photos of you is like staring

at Gene Autry for a long time.
When I close my eyes,
I see your stance gone black
just as his stetson would turn
villainous. No, you didn't
gallop into these pictures.

I put you there to have something
to focus on in the foreground.
Mountains diminish without you for scale.
I was looking for the innuendos of weather:
wedges of dusk on your forehead,
raspberry stained fingers,

gestures of wind through your cowlick.
You can quiver.

My Racy Mind

Lord, thank you for this station.
The DJ preaches so slowly
even sinners can understand Spanish.
Praise the musical confluence
of Highway 5 and my radials.
Forgive me for accepting GPS
as my polestar. It led me
to a belly-up Starbucks.

I beseech thee for relief.
32 beads until the next exit.
Pressure reaching the point
pain will soon be pleasure.
Forgive what the truckers will see
from on high in their semis.
Sweet Jesus! I saw stars for a millisecond.
Now a phalanx of Shivas beckons me,

infinite limbs robed in glossy citrus.
Spare me. Spare them the thrip.
Bless the transubstantiation
of water into Pinot Grigio.
My God. Ganesh is loose in the vineyard.
Trunks dangle from every trellis.
Lift up mine eyes. Lead me over the pass
without overheating. Oh Lordy.

Why must the foothills curve like this?
A commotion of breasts and hips
like India's tantric carvings. Like me.
Bent on tasting oranges and grapes,
swallowing the alpha and omega.
Father. Forgive me my trespasses
as I forgive the barbed wire
for digging its nails in.

Parsing The Body

Without adjectives,
tender will be deleted from love
as will the blood in these oranges.
The veins of purple fingerlings
will become nondescript.

You will not be able to name
the ruffled and bearded irises
or call me luscious,
which also is the scent
where you burrow.

Let's abandon that dictum.
Put your hand here. Tell me
the words on your tongue.
Salty, scarred, erect?
Yes. My breast is

those adjectives.
They come from sweat,
surgery and your touch,
which merits elaboration.
Close your eyes.

Listen to your fingers.
Put them on everything red.
Put them on everything swollen.
Then we will move on
to the verbs and conjunctions.

Pair-Bonding

Sweetheart, nothing undoes me
like watching other couples
dance at weddings.

I feel single
hugging the perimeter
with the widows.

Come on! Open your wingspan.
Flash your iridescence.
I want to dip and soar

and spin and swivel.
Push aside the ground litter.
Bob your topknot.

Do a staccato high step.
Preen me. Nibble my neck.
Feed me your fandango.

Oranges

With all the smudge pots,
who would have thought
they were evergreens?

When you were sixteen,
you lived on crates of Valencias.
Not much left after the rent and gas.

I fell for your ginger hair
the same way birds went for it
during nest building.

It made me think in Spanish—
of the sun falling asleep on my pillow
and the sun waking.

Of *la puesta del sol*
and *el amanecer*.
Of the masculine and feminine.

Of broken chairs that needed a man's touch.
When you came to undo the clamps,
 I offered you red wine so sweet

we added limes and lemons.
Was it the green leaves
of my running shorts

or the night blooming jasmine?
On our first trip, we took the bypass
to collectibles and fruit stands.

That was twenty-five years ago.
I still remember where we pulled over.
All that juice staining us for life.

The Ledge

From the balcony
I can see
deer braving the ridge,
hawks on the railing.

Stairs so steep
I cannot foresee the landing.
Only that someone is there.
Someone to count them with.

There is a rhythm to life
and its infinite series
of cheers and dances.
A syncopation

of hello and goodbye
and hello again.
The twirl out
and the returning.

A belief
that someone is there.
Someone who will right us
no matter how low we dip.

An Honest Moon

for Peter

You say the moon is full
but I say it's almost, even though
it's one of those rare nights
when it was easy to park

near the entrance. Mendelssohn's
Midsummer Night's Dream
isn't holding my attention.
It lacks the dissonance

I feel in your back and neck.
No one on stage is dying.
No voices are wandering,
but my mind is.

I feel intonations of mortality
in each of your knots. Knots that bind us.
This *Wedding March* sugarcoats
life after the recessional.

There's no complacency
in the peignoir. No way
I'll ever enjoy being seen
in something see-through.

I see the future in the widow
we're sharing our picnic with.
Someday only one of us will be left
to remember our coloratura

of accumulation and loss.
The blue dress I wore on our first date.
The heat of the candle wax
the waitress spilled in my lap.

That night we almost broke up —
wearing bibs around our necks,

sucking on crab claws—
because I wanted children.

And all the nights that followed.

III

Our dead are never dead to us,
until we have forgotten them.

George Eliot

Pins

for Beth Sunflower

Pins secured the butterflies
my gentle sister chloroformed.
Every swallowtail still reminds me of her.
They were the darkest and most beautiful.

She knew how to name and order
the *Superfamily Papilionoidea.*
When she was fifteen, she numbed herself
hiding in a trunk full of mothballs.

Not to die. To be safe.
Sometimes the only way to subdue
the world is to stick pins in a map
and migrate.

Every hinge is made of wings and a pin.
A knuckle pulls them together.
I have her brooch with iridescent wings.
When I wear it I remember

how I chased her as she ran with the net,
how I pursued her like nectar.
As if I would morph just by touching
the fragile dust of her.

Nowadays, I notice my hands fluttering
like hers when she was talking.
Every swallowtail reminds me of her.
She was the darkest and most beautiful.

Theft

for Beth and Bob

In the middle of the blackberries
he lets the thorns make him cry
just thinking of all the jam
she will never make again
and all the purple tapestries they wove
twining their stained fingers.

The smell of the sweet river sickens him.
A sickness he did not foresee
as she reached for the ripest branches
in the sunlight. Sunlight
they cracked between their teeth
and spit in the garden.

Their garden of Eden. Her wild sweet peas
camouflaging their perimeter of chain link—
that fence he anchored for protection—
never imagining something inside
could steal her away from him
in the middle of their fertile summer.

Henry Darger's Faith

In the beginning, we were three
and in my mother was life
and it was the light of my father.

Though lightning knew her not,
she was cleaved like a tree
and the word was silence.

And so it came to pass.
My sister entered the world
not by the will of flesh

but by God's hand
though I saw her not —
for she was borne away

in a nun's black sleeve.
Then we were two —
father and son without lullabies.

Nothing green was left for us.
The sun yielded salt,
night consumed us like locusts.

If his light shines in the darkness,
I see it not. For he that makes all things
also takes them.

The Shelf Life of Grief

after a child's suicide

You don't have to worry about losing this.
It's yours forever. This memory
for details. Nights unravelling
never reaching their end.

How your mind does wander.
How you regret the crushed velvet
and plated handles. You paid so much
hoping it would hurt less. Oh yes,

you remember like it was yesterday.
Things you don't want to say. Sometimes
you find yourself halfway across the kitchen
asking, *What is my purpose?*

Small comfort—giving away her clothes
and organs. There are girls her size everywhere.
Now you understand the keening
when they separate dams from their calves.

When your daughter was all hands and knees,
she lay on butcher paper - butcher paper.
The teacher traced her body
like a detective at a crime scene.

Even the good memories
have been twisted by hindsight.
What was God thinking? This was not
the time. This was not the season.

P.O. Box 434

Maybe you're with the eucalyptus smoke.
Or maybe you're sleeping under the redwoods.
I've been cheated. I don't know
where he put you or what box he picked.

You were warm when we last touched.
Your poison oak was healing.
I'd have washed and clothed your body,
spelling out love in the Braille of death.

Kissed you one last time and dressed you
in your fringed sheath and fishnet stockings,
an outfit that conjures up mischief —
and you at twenty, waitressing at the Gaslight.

I've been cheated.
Where are all the clothes that smelled of you?
I don't want them all boxed up.
Don't want everything going to strangers.

 Restless legs and sleep.
Psoriasis and stress.
The healing power of the tango.
Where are your left-handed scissors?

Where are the articles
you never sent? I've been cheated.
Never again will you write
my name in the margins.

Jettison

People shouldn't vanish into thin air
or into the thick of it.
Give me a Captain who says brace yourself.

A Captain who gives me time
to kiss you and choose
what I'm willing to jettison.

Goodbye new shoes and suitcase.
All I need are my glasses to find you.
Don't disappear into a fog

that reminds the hungry
of pea soup, stone soup —
pebbles salting headstones.

Fabric

for Jack Slater

I'm thinking of you
and that phase in your life
when you surprised us all
taking up sewing.

You bought pinking shears
and a tracing wheel,
learned to adjust
the pressure foot.

Your anthurium shirt
could almost hula.
Women were transported
by your tropical cushions.

I hope you kept sewing.
I like to think of you
making curtains,
learning to pleat and gather.

Revelling in the seams
as you pulled them back—
all the bold swatches
in your garden.

Handiwork

for Tina Hodge

David raises his shirt to the light
like a priest raising his chalice.
He kisses each stitch
that you called mending.

He takes comfort
in the wine you made
and the indelible blush
of black currants.

Dust settles in your chair
and your basket of knitting.
Sometimes he lays his head
in its lap and prays

for everything you touched
to come to life again.
For your needles to add sleeves
to his sweater,

for each hinge to swing open,
for the metal to sing
I'm home again.

Swing Low Sweet Chariot

[Robert Curry, PFC]

I love and hate this garage.
I built the hutch for our china here,
sanding each edge for hours.

But my own grain kept rising up
year after year. I yelled at the kids
when they came to watch. Hid

too many bottles of Smirnoff
in my tool chest. I became the man
I ran away from.

When you married me, I was on my way
to France. When I came back, we never talked
about the mud and blood,

all the bodies a medic can't
put back together again. My 30 days
in the brig after I went AWOL.

Here I am—a postman just like my dad,
cheating, drinking up our money.
I'm leaving before I drive you away.

I'm going to join all those soldiers
who floated away from me on ether.
My Chevy's exhaust will carry me to them.

Hope Is a Thing with Feathers

A cat is like a bird
when it is dying.

Its hair lies down
like wet feathers.

It stops flying
to high places.

It hasn't the strength
to preen itself.

We dose it with eye-droppers
the way we nurse chicks

in nests we make
with our fingers.

Nests of sorrow.
Where we must decide

when it is time
to give up on the sparrow.

When it is time to stop
force feeding.

Darting Light

for Patti Brady

Tell me about Tinker Bell.
Why you had her tattooed
on your ankle when you turned fifty.

Why you had them ink
the character for longevity
in place of fairy dust.

You trick me each time
your purple toenails rise.
I forget the pneumatic mattress.

Forget there's no guy wire
to help you fly
or land you safely.

James Barrie believed
in Never Neverland.
He made Tink with a mirror

and a strong light.
He dimmed it when she drank
poison to save Peter.

Told the world that clapping
would bring her back again.
Enough did though some hissed.

Every fairy tale needs its villain.
But not this one. I don't like
the paper gowns and masks.

Don't like pretending.
Why can't the doctors
kill Captain Hook?

Lures

Harvey trolls with science.
His charters guarantee a fish.
The sonar is clear
as any ultrasound.

Sometimes when it's slow,
he cuts the motor and drifts
toward the opaque center.
He's seen his shadow.

He thinks about his wife
and her fear of water.
How she won't watch
when the kids swim,

how she won't look down
crossing the river.
Maybe she knows
something is growing,

something is hungry
beneath the liquid skin.
How deep her love
to wait at the dock for him.

Tuning the Sails

A white nightshirt hangs
from your bony shoulders.
Becalmed, you drool a little,
savoring your words,

loving how they make you
thirsty. Your whole life
you held the shoals
at arm's length —

like a sailor with his witch ball
watching the sirens behind
exhale salty farewells
into a cumulus.

Last night, you heard the sea
breathing. Polished rocks
tumbled in and out
of its great mouth like vowels.

You woke to the pine's shadow
and thought of mizzenmasts.
By dawn, its limbs began singing.
It's time now for your ablutions.

Lick your fingers.
Slick back your wispy hair.
Beg forgiveness
for your white stubble.

Maidenhair Trees

*The genus Ginkgo...dates back to the Lower Jurassic, about 190
million years ago.* — UC Berkeley, Museum of Paleontology

Before we crawled,
we swam.
Before we walked,
we dragged ourselves

through sharp grass
and brackish mud.
We grew red wisps
that the sun dried

and the wind lifted.
Not for warmth or wings,
but for attention
like showy roses.

We found names
for the parts of us
necessary to propagate.
We anointed ourselves

rulers of the kingdom.
Now we think nothing
of killing the female ginkgoes
for reeking in their season.

As if their bodies
weren't made like ours
of oxygen, hydrogen
and carbon.   As if

there were no other
Adam and Eve worth saving.

Four-Letter Words

*for Ed Shneidman, Professor of Thanatology
and Melville Aficionado*

Someday you will wade out
into the slap of the tide
shouting four-letter words
at a vexing cloud of gulls.

Pain. Fear. Hope. Fuck.
Not yet. Not while you
still have some strength left
to fight the sleeper waves.

You still love the way breasts
swell with each inspiration,
the way the old tabby purrs
flexing and unflexing

her perfect paws. Not yet.
Though sometimes in your sleep
you are getting out of your car
and Jeanne is back at the window waiting,

waiting for you to cross
the green grassy sea. Sometimes
you think it will happen
at your desk.

That you will cry out
and drop your pen like an oar.
Or maybe you will drift away
like Melville's white sepulcher

on an azure sea.
You tell me it ends
with two four-letter words —
dead and gone.

No. I say it ends with one —
love.

Notes

P. 17 — "Goethe's Girdle" — Loosely based on a few lines from Goethe's *The Sufferings of Young Werther.*

P. 38 — "Making Sparks" — Found phrases and inspiration taken from the description of fire-building in Kroeber's *Ishi in Two Worlds.*

P. 65 — "Four-Letter Words" — The poem includes a few phrases from Melville's *Moby Dick.*

About the Author

Published in the U.S., Ireland and England, Kita Shantiris' poetry has appeared in *Ambit, Crannóg, Poetry, Quarterly West, The Fish Anthology, The Moth, Slipstream, Wisconsin Review* and other journals. She is one of three poets featured in *The Border* (Bombshelter Press 1984), and two poems were anthologized in *The Faber Book of Movie Verse* (Faber & Faber 1993).

In 2012, she won 2nd Prize in the Ballymaloe International Poetry Contest judged by Leontia Flynn. She twice has been Runner-Up in Fish Publishing's contest judged by Brian Turner (2011) and Ruth Padel (2014).

In her other life, psychologist Dr. Kita S. Curry runs Didi Hirsch Mental Health Services, a non-profit in Los Angeles. For that work, she has been honored for erasing stigma and bringing services to communities of color.

Her website is *www.kitashantiris.com.*

Other Recent Titles from Mayapple Press:

Devon Moore, *Apology from a Girl Who Is Told She Is Going to Hell,* 2015
        Paper, 84pp, $15.95 plus s&h
        ISBN 978-1-936419-54-8
Sara Kay Rupnik, *Women Longing to Fly,* 2015
        Paper, 102pp, $15.95 plus s&h
        ISBN 978-1-936419-50-0
Jeannine Hall Gailey, *The Robot Scientist's Daughter,* 2015
        Paper, 84pp, $15.95 plus s&h
        ISBN 978-936419-42-5
Jessica Goodfellow, *Mendeleev's Mandala,* 2015
        Paper, 106pp, $15.95 plus s&h
        ISBN 978-936419-49-4
Sarah Carson, *Buick City,* 2015
        Paper, 68pp, $14.95 plus s&h
        ISBN 978-936419-48-7
Carlo Matos, *The Secret Correspondence of Loon and Fiasco,* 2014
        Paper, 110pp, $16.95 plus s&h
        ISBN 978-1-936419-46-3
Chris Green, *Resumé,* 2014
        Paper, 72pp, $15.95 plus s&h
        ISBN 978-1-936419-44-9
Paul Nemser, *Tales of the Tetragrammaton,* 2014
        Paper, 34pp, $12.95 plus s&h
        ISBN 978-1-936419-43-2
Catherine Anderson, *Woman with a Gambling Mania,* 2014
        Paper, 72pp, $15.95 plus s&h
        ISBN 978-1-936419-41-8
Victoria Fish, *A Brief Moment of Weightlessness,* 2014
        Paper, 132pp, $16.95 plus s&h
        ISBN 978-1-936419-40-1
Susana H. Case, *4 Rms w Vu,* 2014
        Paper, 72pp, $15.95 plus s&h
        ISBN 978-1-936419-39-5
Elizabeth Genovise, *A Different Harbor,* 2014
        Paper, 76pp, $15.95 plus s&h
        ISBN 978-1-936419-38-8

For a complete catalog of Mayapple Press publications, please visit our website at *www.mayapplepress.com.* Books can be ordered direct from our website with secure on-line payment using PayPal, or by mail (check or money order). Or order through your local bookseller.